THE
TAKEAWAY

A RAUCOUS TALE ABOUT
THE ART OF THE SALE

By John Lewis Evans Jr

ISBN: 9781796811636

The author disclaims responsibility for adverse effects or consequences from the misapplication or injudicious use of the information contained in this book. Mention of resources and associations does not imply an endorsement.

Scriptor
PUBLISHING GROUP

This book is dedicated to John Michael Night, my hero.

A portion of the proceeds will go wherever he wants.

Proceeds will also go to the Janus Henderson Foundation.

Praise for *The Takeaway*

"I have now read this book 3x. Each time I have gotten more and more out of it that I can apply to our industry. I have more notes in the margin of my printed copy than you can possibly imagine. I am in the Villages about to have a meeting with our staff and it is the foundation of our meeting. But I am doing it in small groups. Digging in. Asking each the questions. The impact that it has had with the small groups I have done so far, I cannot even express in words. Our team has grown up in our culture and values especially out here in the Villages so they get looking for ways to delight our Guests and catching each other doing this right. But you have taken our core to NEXT LEVEL!!! As I am writing this text I am getting goosebumps!!!"

– Gina Buell

Founder, City Fire American Oven & Bar
Franchisee Florida, Wahlburgers

"Underlying the incredible humor and intensely gratifying storytelling, John Evans has woven in some true lessons on life, learning, and the art and science of sales. A must read for anyone in sales, considering sales, or simply for those who want a hearty, belly laugh."

– Michael Ehret, PhD

VP of Human Resources, Johnson & Johnson

"A fabulous fun-filled story that provides many golden nuggets from a new, important genre: 'instructional humor.'"

– Jeff Singletary

Keller Williams Heritage Realty

"This book is not only a hoot, but it will improve sales. Finally someone has captured the intensity, insanity and absurdity of selling and salesmanship, all the while serving up some important nuggets that just might make each of us a wee bit better at sales ourselves. And if everyone buys in to the critical message, it will improve something else more valuable—your team's culture. Just as important, like Owen, I laughed so hard, I nearly peed."

– Mark Freid

President, Think Creative Inc.

"Dr. Evans provides a hilarious narrative framework that will give your sales team a common language to build successful culture—and hit their sales targets. Buy it for your whole team and let the learning begin!"

– Richard J. Clarke

Chief Strategy, Sales and Marketing Officer
Del-Air Heating and Air Conditioning

"Assuming the student is wholehearted about her product or service, Dr. J. is masterful and well-crafted in this whimsical

tale on how everyone and anyone can sell anything."

– Sheri Lacasse
Manager, U.S. Intermediary Channel Marketing
Global Financial Service Company

"The Takeaway is brilliantly written. It distills important leadership, sales, and life principles into a fictional story that keeps you laughing and learning the whole way through. The story held my attention with its pop culture references, short chapters, and dynamic character development. Its central theme of making moments of meaning is powerful and truly transformative to the traditional sales approach. I definitely recommend it."

– Shannon Fletcher, Ed.D.
Associate Professor in the College of Business
Northwest University

"This book is scary good. Win others over, and learn to Woo Well. Be well-rounded, literally and figuratively. Play an instrument and speak two languages. Always smile. Stomach in and shoulders back. 99% percent of it: showing up. Enjoy the journey. Nothing comes between me and my Calvin Kleins. Now, most importantly, get ready to laugh out loud at Evans' treasure."

– Elana Tabachnikov,
Executive Recruiter, TAOS

"I remember going to my first sales training class and realizing what I was learning did not resonate. Now I know why. This book explains what anyone who sells anything needs to know. It's a great mix of humor along with an important message, and it turns out EVERYONE is in sales."

– Mark Magnacca
President and Co-Founder, Allego

"The essence of sales is storytelling, and no one does it better than John Evans. Here, he has his oversized cast of characters take us on a hilarious and insightful ride all the way to the intersection of income and integrity. A must read for rookies and journeymen alike!"

– Sandy Modell
Hedge Fund G.P./Adj. Prof.

"This read is fabulous with vivid details and loveable characters! A new favorite for sales coaching and story-selling that outshines its peers who are drowning in a sea of sameness. Epic!"

– Meg Daker
Sales Trainer, Global Financial Service Company

"Humor has serious potential to transform how we think, feel and act - strengthening connections and making memories that last. For anyone serious about creating a tremendous

client experience, The Takeaway will not only have them laughing out loud, it'll have them laughing all the way to the bank!"

-Heidi Hanna, Ph.D.
-NY Times Best Selling Author
Executive Director of The American Institute of Stress

"The Takeaway should be required reading for every young person embarking on a career in business. John Evans takes you on an entertaining journey that provides remarkable insights on how charisma and drive may produce short term results, but one can only find true success through devotion and service to others both in business and in life."

-Brian Blackburn
Founder & C.E.O
XYMOGEN, Inc

"Good grief. To see all of this in print after I've been hearing about it on my office couch for years is really something…and it is very, very valuable."

-Robert Goldstein, M.D.
The Author's Psychiatrist

This book is written for every poor sap who has
had to endure a day of terrible sales training.

From your family to your nation, and all organizations
in between, culture is king. May this tall tale contribute
in some small way, or otherwise, to the cultures
in which you find yourself.

For additional resources and expanded content, please visit:
TheTakeawayBook.com/Resources

Table of Contents

CHAPTER 1:   The Gaze 1

CHAPTER 2:   The Sales Contest 7

CHAPTER 3:   Let's Play Ball, Murdoch 9

CHAPTER 4:   A Shorn Lamb 23

CHAPTER 5:   Just Clean That Shot Glass, Sweetie 27

CHAPTER 6:   An Upward Spiral of Positivity 31

CHAPTER 7:   Champagne Bottles Everywhere 35

CHAPTER 8:   The Lost Art of the Exit...................................37

CHAPTER 9:   God Rest Pa's Soul 43

CHAPTER 10: MOMM..45

CHAPTER 11: An Inkling...59

CHAPTER 12: It's a Horror Show...63

CHAPTER 13: Groovin'...69

CHAPTER 14: Angels Singing 73

CHAPTER 15: Longhorn Shot Glass, Airborne........................77

CHAPTER 16: Chung Suffers No Fools....................................79

CHAPTER 17: Vital, and Incidental...81

CHAPTER 18: "You Don't Know
                    What the Hell You're Missing" 83

CHAPTER 19: Defend Richmond...89

CHAPTER 20: Red Dot Above Kneecap...................................99

Discussion Topics for Business Development Teams 103

Acknowledgments 105

CHAPTER 1

The Gaze

A short, furry, ferocious man took the stage at The Orlando Timeshare Hut, with an unmistakable sense of urgency. He was comical at first glance. (Think athletic Danny DeVito. Think honey badger.) Neanderthal-like, with enormous haunches. As his football coach at Yale remarked decades prior, "He had a high rump perfect for the power needed to play nose guard."

He was the boss, and his gaze to the audience of 250 "sales associates" from his timeshare company behemoth said as much. In fact, that gaze was a thing of legend; it stopped folks in their tracks. You found yourself in a curious state when his brown eyes locked into yours. He never used PowerPoint, calling it the biggest sham in the history of persuasion and business development. Maybe an image or two on the screen, but that's it. His eyes were the only projectors he needed. His energy level seemed boundless, of high quality, and ignited by an uncommon sense of purpose. Listeners didn't know it, but for 30 minutes before his speeches, the timeshare industry patriarch would rest almost motionless, like a great lion on the African plain, managing his energy with full intention. But when the moment came and he took the stage . . . you, the listener, were going to do whatever he wanted. It was a God-given attribute, his speech giving—then sculpted, curated, and fine-tuned from tireless intention and grit.

For the powerful 5-foot-6 furry fellow, draped in a fair amount of gold, age was simply not a variable in the personal narrative. Only energy mattered—the supreme asset. Before every single talk he had ever given, he asked himself this question and answered it before storming the stage: "So what? Why should anyone listen to a lick of what I am about to say?" Furthermore, he reminded himself with impeccable discipline, that the speech was never about him. Rather, it was about the betterment of his audience. Mulling this theme enlivened the time-share miniature giant time and time again before his speech delivery. The kernels of advice came from his great-grandpappy, Otis, a carpetbagging former Union soldier-turned-charlatan salesman of snake oil and other fine things in life.

He took the stage winsomely.

"I drove down here on U.S. Highway 1, from Brockton, Massachusetts, to Orlando after the war and almost attaining my fancy degree. I had $177 in my pocket, half a box of cigars, and a lousy Rottweiler named Okeechobee Hank. That's all I had. *(Pause.)* Along with a gut full of 'want to.'"

The sales associates had heard this part of the speech before, and no worries, they would love hearing it again. All were spellbound, including a janitor.

"But I ain't happy right now!" He continued his speech with a growl, slight scratch to the groin, and counterbalancing optimistic dispatch of eyebrows, upward. The otherwise sprightly, plucky salespeople hushed with haste. Their alpha was speaking; it was time to suspend the chirps of complaints, gossips, and exultations. They were convening in their world-renowned timeshare sales facility in south Orlando known as The Hut. The architecture was bold, gold, and ornate. Attractive assistants with chiseled derrières and full chests passed out protein-rich chia smoothies. A communicative genius, Funk continued with the most important persuasion tool ever given to God's great showroom floor: a story.

"Look. Sales suck. They suck. If you want to get anywhere in life, whether it's to Sacramento, to VP of Sales, or into someone's undergarments, you've got to face truth. We're facing it right now. Airbnb is kicking our tail."

Another pause to the speech, manufacturing a moment. In his astoundingly long and distinguished career as a public speaker, CEO Elliot Funkhauzer, known affectionately to all as Funk, was a huge fan of the gaze, staring down individual members of his time-share-selling juggernaut and memorizing how they'd respond to his hot, silent pressure. If you folded your arms or demurred, he'd remember. He'd also remember the faces of those who alighted, whose body language perked up to the formidable stimulus of his speech. One such sales notoriety, with shoulders broadened and eyebrows up, was Nick Fontaigne. Nick and others would be the chosen ones as the earnings before interest, taxes, and amortization would rise. And EBITA always rose at the firm over the decades.

Until now.

In his speech delivery, Funk was acutely aware of the power of his hands. Though his stature was only 5-foot-6—okay, 5-foot-9 because of his custom shoe guy from Vogel Shoes, Brooklyn Navy Yard—he seemed much bigger when speaking. A lot of that was due to his hands, enormous and striking. These things had helped him move the center from Harvard or Cornell to wherever he wanted to put him. They had grabbed .50-caliber guns on his anti-kamikaze warship in the South Pacific and, over the last decades, had served him well in giving electric speeches to big-motored salespeople. Like a maestro presiding over his symphony, Funk directed his listeners with his outsized paws—they were his batons—as they complemented each word or sound effect emanating from his big mouth and booming voice.

Back to a three-sentence story, the elixir to move his people and sales, and then to an edict.

"I built this company on guts and grit and bullshit. The good kind of BS—the kind that uplifts and inspires, like a Sylvester Stallone movie.

"I am here to announce a brand-new sales contest that promises to fire up this company again—to make it great once more—feared by all those other loser, knock-off timeshare companies that offer pathetic products that'll never get your customers to the likes of Cancun or Breckenridge or the east side of Malaysia, where the prettiest ladies are. No, I haven't been a great leader for you lately; the death of my granddaughter overtook me. But I am back, and *we are back*. Y'all haven't had the best product set to sell, but now you do. Let's roll."

The great CEO quietly blanched after his last comments. Years and years of leadership delivery were furnishing some wisdom. He knew he had to add a dash of vulnerability in each of his speeches now. Not too much, mind you, but a genuine nugget about how you suffered and are bouncing back. This always had genuine impact on his peeps. You also had to express sincere empathy for your peeps' plight and point the way forward. Big Shooter Funk never had a problem pointing the way forward. Whether it was leading his gang of misfits on the streets of Brockton, Massachusetts, growing up, or in the Battle of the Coral Sea in World War II, or through a timeshare sales slump like at present, he always saw the way.

He didn't know it at the time, but the vivacious octogenarian was about to have another growth spurt.

Okeechobee Hank IV

CHAPTER 2

The Sales Contest

Funkhauzer's grandson was unaccomplished. Owen's life was culminating as a collection of undifferentiated, advanced juvenile activities, centered exclusively on his personal titillation. The proverbial privileged millennial (think Owen Wilson) was utterly spunkless unless dueling in the latest generation of Fortnight. He had worked in HR for his grandfather's firm, adding no value. He was rather pathetic if not for his sensational girlfriend, Marianne McKay, from PR.

When the announcement of the sales contest came, it struck Owen like a freight train. He remembered the chilling morning, 26 years prior, when on a family vacation in northwestern Maine, his Grandpa Funk had thrown him in Mooselookmeguntic Lake to teach him how to swim. Owen was four.

"Sink or swim, kid. It's how the world works."

For the entirety of his life, Owen had been trying to escape that feeling, to numb it out. Now the horror narrative was back in spades with the announcement. The demon had returned in full splendor.

Then it appeared. Up and out of the ether, like a dagger from hell. A tweet from his brand-new and first-ever nemesis, Nick Fontaigne:

> *"Roses are red, I got some glue. The smell of loser is stuck on you."*

Nick had just heard about the sales contest, an event that would change his career trajectory. And not a moment too soon, in his mind. He'd been selling the Platinum Premium packages like an absolute banshee. Frankly, it was high time the mothership acknowledged his talent.

Funkhauzer had proclaimed that there would be a two-year sales contest to boost energy and revenue in his global firm. Fontaigne would be moving to Shanghai in two weeks and would start team assembly immediately; grandson, Owen, to Paris. The world was divided in half. Whoever drove the most sales in the two-year period would become SVP of Global Marketing for the firm. What a prize! It was on, baby. *Sink or swim, boys. It's how the world works.* Tête à tête, mano a mano.

Owen nearly peed.

CHAPTER 3

Let's Play Ball, Murdoch

Nick Fontaigne grew up hardscrabble. Ancestry. com informed him that, a few generations ago, his Southern ancestors were heroes of the Civil War. They were fabulously wealthy, but as some version of the saying goes, when the third generation comes around, the money's somehow nowhere to be found.

Fontaigne wanted it back, along with his prestigious French-American name. He had watched a video by some cocky Yankee named Simon Sinek, and it fired him up. Most salespeople knew what they sold and how they sold it. Fontaigne went a step further. He had come to understand *why* he sold timeshare—FAMILY PRESTIGE RESTORATION. He could completely sympathize with the great Big Shooter Funk's feverish desire to restore the company. Likewise, Fontaigne wanted to make his family great again. Selling timeshare was the vehicle for family regentrification.

With the sales contest his ship was in the harbor, and there was absolutely no frickin' possible way on God's green earth he would be defeated by some nose-picking grandson of the founder. No way! His instincts immediately engulfed him, and he began the process of intimidation of Owen. He wasn't being a bully; this is simply how the world worked. Just watch *National Geographic Wild*; either the hyena or the lion would get the gazelle. Not both. The predator with the most fight and the best bite, wins.

Nick had plenty of fight. After reading a life-changing book by one of the country's leading trial attorneys entitled *You Can't Teach Hungry*, Nick was on fire. But he also had to work on his strategy, his bite.

Selling timeshare required a particular bite. Nobody needed the product. Potential buyers were typically sitting in front of you because they had been bribed to do so with an assortment of freebies: gaming chips, tickets to a show, or maybe points on their reward system. The hunter needed a well-thought-out plan, or process, to get his prey to separate from his money. After all, they would be dropping thousands upon thousands of dollars that day, and they would not be able to enjoy their new product for weeks and weeks. And they were buying time, for goodness' sake. What is that?

Over the years of earning outsized bonus checks, Fontaigne was learning from the heat of the marketplace. There were no ribbons issued by his sales manager for trying hard. No, if you sold, you ate. If you didn't, you didn't. That simple. Pure meritocracy. Fontaigne thrived in this environment. His central nervous system had been forming in-kind over the years. When he closed a Platinum Premium package, dopamine and oxytocin were secreted into his bloodstream. He got amped. And he had a corresponding ritual. Every time he sold a premium package, he would take his prized, inherited cannon, called "The Hell Yeah" from the Battle of Atlanta (his ancestor had used this weapon to fight off Yankees), and fire the enormous gun outside his ranch in Lubbock, Texas. A rebel yell might emerge too. His dog, Razzmatazz, outsized even by Great Dane standards, was gold. His master had selected him as a pup for his enormous testicles and a thunderclap bark that would eventually create reverberations from the countless first-place medal sales trophies that Fontaigne would accumulate over the years. The soft hum of the medals after the bark was the sound that gave Master Fontaigne deep satisfaction.

Every single morning for the last five years, Fontaigne arose with the sun, irrespective of the enormity of his hangover. He sat down at his glass table and fine-tuned the operating structure for the most successful selling process of timeshare, or nearly anything else, ever devised. He knew, *really knew*, that this process would punch his ticket to his career, bring him millions, and reinstate the glory of the Fontaigne name. He was also keenly aware that the framework had to be simple and easy to implement for new sales associates so it could be scaled.

Heaven Almighty! Here it was:

The 5D Sales Process

1. Detain the client
2. Disorient
3. Dominate
4. Demand
5. Down payment

Detain the client: The author of the curriculum had learned that he must have full control over his prospect. Undivided attention. He would witness the prospect's turning off of the smartphone. There had to be full fealty to the master sales trainer extraordinaire. The room was locked down, with no windows. Attractive and perfectly appointed, the "closing station" was to induce full engagement with the trainer. Nobody, *nobody*, was to come near the closing station unless it was planned.

Disorient the client: Here's where Fontaigne took his cue from the *National Geographic Wild* TV show again. Studying how predators took down their prey, there was always surprise—getting the victim off his guard, unbalanced. It was critical to understand that he was listening as much as he was talking during this part of his manipulative process. Engaging with the nice couple from Wichita, he was sifting for clues. *What was happening with the couple that could be exploited?* He knew they had come into the meeting to get the free gaming chips, and they had made a pact, more than likely, to not purchase timeshare. This mindset required ferocious disruption. Unhinge the conservative Murdochs from Wichita. Off balance, like the Ethiopian gazelle, induced to find itself cornered at the base of a rocky cliff. Once, in a customary lightning-quick scan of Twitter before sitting down with his prospects, the master had learned the couple were passionate pet lovers. Fontaigne feigned overwhelming grief over the fictitious story of Razzmatazz nearly losing his leg in a bizarre lawn mower accident with the neighbor. "I had just gotten home to the ranch after an unbelievable day at the office. I had liberated an enormous family from the bondage of renting their vacations from hotels—kept them from being ripped off! There were champagne bottles everywhere from our celebration of their decision. I pulled in my driveway, and my hippy neighbor, who was wearing a bandana *(pronounced slowly and emphatically to communicate hippiness)*, was completely mindless and ran over my doggie's foot. And *(parenthetically added as soft as a feather)* the driver of the lawn mower had been a socialist Bernie Sanders supporter." The Murdochs were overcome with sorrow and anger—the sweet Great Dane had been maimed by an emissary of the monster himself, Bernie. Now they were ready to listen to whatever Nick Fontaigne had to say.

A little voice, energizing like soft, red lightning, crept into Fontaigne's consciousness, as it always did in this part of 5D . . . *Fontaigne makes rain.*

Dominate the client: Now Fontaigne had them. He was in the throes of the dance between empathy and assertion, arousing emotional energy with apparent sincerity. The lawn mower story had done its work. Now it was time to get radical—to unleash a storm as to how pernicious and ruthless the hotel chains, boutiques, and internet options were in taking your money over the years and leaving you with nothing. The Rent vs. Own vacation deconstruction was brought to light. You were being ripped off renting your vacations. Now, it was time for the savior to show you how you could own your vacations. Have a deed. Get yourself some of the American dream. The prospects were to be overwhelmed with the force of argument.

"Just what the hell do you have after 30 years of renting your vacations? Answer: You ain't got squat." With a pound of the desk and eyeballs at full radiance, Fontaigne was good here, masterful. His finely tuned data-gathering collection mechanism, during the course of the engagement, informed him whether he should proceed with more logic or emotion. If, say, the alpha of the dyad was a high school math instructor, he would hammer home the dollars and cents being thrown away in the garbage can to hotels and Airbnb. If the couple leaned more toward a creative, artistic bend, he would carry on about the evils of the hotel industry. If eyes were windows to the soul, Fontaigne knew eyebrows were the shades—eyebrows would come down with the signaling of evil hotels and Airbnb. Call it the "condemnational" eyebrow deployment.

He was continually looking for the distinction between interests and positions as he moved to the closing of the timeshare deal. Nick was loaded for bear for the predictable positions to be hurled his way: "The time just isn't right"; or, "We are waiting on a big promotion"; or, "We need to think about it." These were all positions which may or not reflect the buyer's interests, particularly that third response. It was as expected as a Texas dust storm.

"We need to think about it, before we plunk down $32,000, and that amount, incidentally, represents 20% of our gross annual income."

Of course, the couple should think about it.

But that response just wouldn't do for Fontaigne and his regentrifying name campaign. He would be so poised to pounce on this comment, poised to dominate, and he would certainly deploy one of the greatest interpersonal manipulative tools ever devised:

The Takeaway.

"Gosh, Mrs. Murdoch," as his hand slowly but forcefully moved to take all the pretty brochures away, off the table and out of reach for his prey. Images of Cancun, Stockholm, and the sun-setting hills of Albuquerque were to vanish.

With full passive aggression distributed by a tone he had worked to master for years, Fontaigne delivered the invective—quintessential passive aggression.

Vacation ownership wasn't for everybody. "*Frankly, there are two types of people in this world, Mr. and Mrs. Murdoch: thinkers and doers. Clearly, y'all are thinkers. That's cool.*"

In an instant, all glitzy PR material disappeared from the table. The Murdoch's passions and interests were stripped. This was not to be for them. The dazzling emissary of the timeshare behemoth was pointing out, underhandedly, that they were not good enough to be part of the club. Mr. Murdoch felt physically stunted, like the time he was cut from the high school baseball team. And that team's star pitcher, by the way, happened to resemble Fontaigne in so many ways. The pain of rejection was returning. He was not going to be on the team.

Existential burn. Murdoch tried to calmly mull the mantra presented by Psychiatrist Goldstein, "When the burn returns—and we all have one, by the way—you must *respond*, not *react*." Stay calm and reflect. Assess the narratives showing forth.

But one of Murdoch's voices, well, dominated ...

"Damn, Nick's right. I have given so much money to hotels, renting them over the years. What do I have to show for that money?" He pondered. "Some lousy points and faint memories. And hell, they were going, too. Ugh, his Uncle Vernon's dementia—did it run in the family? Mr. Fontaigne was spot on: I had no deed to my vacations. Nothing to pass on to my sweet three grandchildren."

"Just hold on a minute, Nick," said Mr. Murdoch from Wichita, Kansas. "Just how much do I have to put down today?"

Mrs. Murdoch squirmed as Nick continued to walk away from the table.

Perfectly timed, a breathtaking assistant suddenly appeared and announced, "The Arrisson's are back again, at Table 5, to purchase their second Double Platinum package; this one's for their grandchildren!" Fontaigne pretended to start making his way to Table 5—also known as, when the situation called for it, the Gateway to the Doers Club.

The Takeaway was now in full detonation, in grand splendor, and unforgiving. Human beings desperately crave to be part of a club—the craving is among the most powerful forces in human experience. The master knew of this phenomenon on a deeper level than any academic psychologist or anthropologist could ever convey; Nick lived it in the fire of a wrenching marketplace. Do you destroy and consume the gazelle, or do you not?

Fontaigne pretended not to hear the question, "How much?" Further, he pretended to make a comment to an assistant, pretending to be out of earshot of Mr. Murdoch, knowing full well the power of the bomb. "Close the Murdoch file, Annabelle."

The interpersonal manipulative pièce de résistance, a hairy knuckled heart punch, just too much to bear . . . *Close the file.*

"Just how much do I have to put down today, Fontaigne?" the emerging new club member barked for the second time, with a hint of desperation. Damned if he was going to *not* be a part of another team in his life— not one that promised so much joy, like that baseball team. And this vacation ownership opportunity, that was so sweet a deal.

"For you, Mr. Murdoch, it's only 15K today. Congratulations on becoming a Platinum owner today. You won't regret it." *(Handshake and kiss to cheek of wife.)*

"Annabelle will be right in with the paperwork." The beautiful assistant swept in, her entire comportment changing from imperious, distant executive assistant, to

Olivia Newton John in the movie, *Grease.* *"You are going to LOOOOVE being timeshare members."*

Next, the master would matriculate to the next phase of the sales process, demanding down payment. The force was so great at this point with the Murdochs. Every fiber of Fontaigne's being was assuming the full $15,000 deposit would be produced NOW; the perfectly appointed Canali suit with apricot-colored Brooks Brothers dress shirt and no tie, permitting display of a few select chest hairs to celebrate Fontaigne virility, conveyed professional urgency. Absolutely right now the money must move. Not tomorrow, and certainly not next week.

Fontaigne was all too familiar with the marketing data. If this couple walked out of The Hut without making the investment, then "Fuhgettabout 'em," as Yankees would say. They'd be gone, back to the expansive African plain, never to be seen again. No, sir! The lion would be collecting his meat right now.

The 15K appeared in the form of a strained Murdoch Mastercard.

Contracts appeared, lightning-like. "Press hard, three copies," said Annabelle.

In 30 seconds, Nick penned a handwritten congratulations letter that would appear in the Murdoch's Kansas mailbox in a strategic three days, when they could still rescind the deal. Nick acknowledged them for being doers. The baseball story had come up over coffee after the paperwork had been signed, in the post-deal relaxation and affirmation chamber. Nick took account of the information. His personal letter concluded, "Let's play ball, Murdoch."

In the meantime, the deal was done. The lion had fed. PayPal moved proceeds as expeditiously as a breath. Nick would never see the Murdochs again, nor dimly want to. Annabelle patted Nick's rump twice in a customary congratulatory gesture, celebrating teamwork. The appletini would soon taste as delicious as always at *Happy Hour at The Hut.*

.

CHAPTER 4

A Shorn Lamb

Owen was sick. It was the anniversary of the death of his sister, Alexandria. She was "The Chosen One." Grandpa Funk loved her the most, and he said so. She had her grandfather's overwhelming charisma and her mother's height and hair. She could stop a clock and put a spell on you. It was only right and natural that she was being groomed to take over the firm.

If only she'd not gone to that sales celebration party in Daytona and had survived the Interstate 4 head-on crash created by the unwitting killer who felt compelled to text an urgent, lengthy joke to his friend while at the wheel.

The depth of the family shattering was vast. Darkness came. Grandpa Funk took it the hardest. Inconsolable and stationary for two straight weeks, he was struck to the core. He managed to get to the funeral, and for some reason, a parenthetical remark by the pastor made its way inside him, however meekly. "The Almighty is terribly interested in how we respond in our darkest hour, and know that *He will temper the wind to the shorn lamb*." Funk was beyond shorn; he was raw.

Owen, having moved to Paris to lead the European theatre of the timeshare contest, could not get any momentum with his sales training. The anniversary of his sister's death hung over him like a cold, damp wool blanket. Insults to his mood included Snapchats of the 5D, which were everywhere on the internet. But he couldn't get his selling team to use this method. Down deep, or perhaps not even that deep, he knew it was manipulation. It was wrong. Who cares how "successful" the 5D was, if morally repugnant? Owen was down, and almost out. A dark, dark hour. He could not escape a recurring nightmare of being eaten alive by an anaconda from Amarillo. Head first.

Oh, he missed his sister dearly.

There must be a better way.

Marianne McKay had an idea. She, too, was tired of hearing of Fontaigne's 5D Sales Process. Crafting countless PR announcements defending the sales tactic on Twitter were beginning to grate on her. When she hit Send on the dozens of defenses, she'd promptly get the feeling of being a slimeball. She believed in the firm and cherished her role managing social media, but something had to give. Oh, and the emergence of actual legal entities that would "emancipate" timeshare owners from their dreaded contracts, was troubling.

Moreover, her boyfriend had to win this contest; ambition was no stranger to Ms. McKay. But how? Fontaigne was dominating with the sales numbers two months in. The texts were unremitting from Fontaigne to her emasculated mate:

"Do you squat to pee, O?"

"Roses are red, your socks are pink. I am quite sure, you're as pathetic as I think."

"Enjoying your sweet lattes in Paris, Monsieur Wussinheim?"

Or the pièce de résistance: "Been swimming in northern Maine lately?" (with emoji of swimmer going under).

How did he know?

Just like the time he floundered in the deep, cold lake of northern Maine, Owen Funkhauzer was painfully lost again—in a panic state. He had no vision for a way out. For a road to victory. He had just enough business acumen to realize the necessity of a plan; clarity, indeed, was power. He just had no idea where to turn.

CHAPTER 5

Just Clean That Shot Glass, Sweetie

She was a long, grand beauty with deep brown eyes. (Think Bonnie Raitt, boasting dark red hair with complementing dashes of silver.) Well built from ranch work, dignified, and a bit imperious, her selection and appointment of diamonds perfectly suited. Said this way, all eyes in a room had to go her way. She was fine with that.

One man in her life had outsized influence. Mary Elizabeth Tabachnikov's father, a Russian-Jewish immigrant known for being able to do long division in his head and to recite considerable swaths of Slavic literature, was bigger than life. Standing 6-foot-5, he was the thrill of the party. No, he *was* the party. He had opinions on everything, *absolutely* everything. But his abiding intellectual passion was the art and science of persuasion. Mikhail was curious, deeply curious, about how any person could convince any other person to do anything. His family having escaped Nazi Germany, he settled on a professorial role in the Appalachian backcountry. There he met fire—his wife, Priscilla Hobbs, a Scotch-Irish, red-headed country gal who assembled the first women's boxing league. (Think Reba McIntyre.) These two married and produced Mary Elizabeth, or Mary. The couple was a thing of beauty for their adoring daughter, and so many others, particularly Mary's friends. Mikhail loved to make his daughter's friends appear in the best light, as their best selves. Before one of his famous parties at their country home, he would play Mozart Symphony No. 40 in G Minor on his violin, alone for the friend, ensuring the young, shy gal learned the precise identity of the song. Then later, just as the party hit full tilt, he would play the song and ask the young friend to identify it, with full attention and spotlight from the delighted partygoers. The young gal shone, with her proper song ID. The crowd went berserk. Mikhail would then promptly dive into an electrifying version of Charlie Daniels' "The Devil Went Down to Georgia" to keep his guests from the Deep South—many of whom were quite simpler than their host—enthralled.

Mary grew up hearing lectures at the dining room table on the virtues of persuasion and why it mattered.

"You are here on God's green earth to have effect!" Mikhail would exhort to his family, pounding his fist on the table. "Every great person persuaded well." Then silence, with a dramatic, though measured, sip of Appalachian whiskey—moonshine, in fact. "But it's what's in your heart that matters." Then *wham*, another slug to the table and an according belch, that wouldn't seem inappropriate. "It's what's in your heart that matters. Take care of your flock, whoever that might be." One more time, softer now with the mighty fist, for impact.

"Just clean that shot glass when you're through, my sweet Cossack tough guy," deadpanned Priscilla. She could always persuade him successfully. Undefeated, in fact, over decades of an iconic marriage.

Mary adored her father and mother. And she adored her country. Where else would two more colorful parents, with entirely different gene pools, assemble?

CHAPTER 6

An Upward Spiral of Positivity

Mary Elizabeth showed up for work at Tupperware. Sales were just starting to expand. The products were revolutionizing how food was stored. Mary recognized straightaway that she was in business when she saw her mother's face light up upon utility of the product—properly securing local venison, for a long winter ahead.

Given her lifelong lectures on persuasion from Papa, the Great, and a product she believed in wholeheartedly, she was off to the races in her marketing career, consistently finding herself atop the selling board at the burgeoning firm.

But she was beginning to learn something of over-the-top value. If she would go beyond the business at hand with her clients, then systematically, like clockwork, magic started to happen professionally and personally. For example, one day after another successful sales call, she noticed a lady was struggling, worrying about her son's ability to get a job. Mary looked at the 18-year-old's resume; it was a mess. Being an expert communicator, Mary sat down with the boy and made improvements to the resume. Lo and behold, the lad landed a job shortly thereafter. How did the mother respond? With the biggest "WOW!" Mary Elizabeth had ever heard. And, a teardrop.

Then, something curious happened. The lady picked up the phone and started calling people—telling them about Mary and her product. Business skyrocketed, as Mary Elizabeth learned that there is no greater marketing vessel than a wowed client. Importantly, Mary started having more fun than ever in her life. She didn't know it at the time, but the heightened happiness was actually becoming her strategic advantage in a marketplace getting more crowded by the day. *She was creating a beautiful culture for her clients and associates, an upward spiral of positivity.* People want to be part of a great culture, of upward spirals.

From that resume-improvement moment forward, she would resolve to deliver a moment of meaning to every client in her business world. Whatever the situation lent her, she resolved to be intentional, to make meaning for her flock, as Pa would emphatically have it.

Eighteen months later, she would go on to earn more than the CEO.

CHAPTER 7

Champagne Bottles Everywhere

T he 5D was settling in nicely in Shanghai. Nick's selling team was killing it. One late afternoon they sat down at The Wolfpack Shanghai bar and grill. "Look y'all," he would say to small groups of Chinese time-share prospects, as his managers would listen in and take feverish notes. "This program is not for everyone. I know you all might still be a little bitter about the outcome of WWII, but heck, here's a chance to get a little piece of the American dream."

The master salesman's dunderhead remark was dismissed by the assembly of middle-class businesspeople, electrified by the energy of this large American amalgam of Clint Eastwood and Will Ferrell. They were in—and not going to miss out on their chance to join a timeshare club.

Fontaigne's sales training classes were becoming a thing of lore.

"Champagne bottles were everywhere," Nick told his prey. "This family from Zhejiang Province *(pronounced completely incorrectly)* bought so many Platinum packages that we couldn't help but bring out cases of champagne to celebrate with the family."

Like the parental lion playing with a maimed gazelle for instruction to offspring, Nick was modeling storytelling for his observing fledgling sales managers. Never mind if the story had its facts a little off-kilter. It was all about effect! Stir souls. Activate them to be part of the club. And always, *always*, have the takeaway at the ready, to appeal to the base nature of club membership of his potential buyers.

Nick was firing off The Hell Yeah cannon almost daily with the business success, and Razzmatazz was right there, howling all the while. Young Chinese sales associates simply couldn't get enough of it. "My people invented dynamite," exhorted one promising and admiring sales associate from Wuhan.

"That's nice."

Chapter 8

The Lost Art of the Exit

Mary Elizabeth agreed to the meeting with her niece and the distressed business development manager. She'd always loved Marianne, encouraging her in her career, and it was a wonderful coincidence the two found themselves in Paris together.

The three met at a café near a fashionable neighborhood in the famed Sacré-Coeur district. Owen felt dragged to the meeting, but at this point he was pretty much desperate. Professionally he felt like he was dying, letting his grandfather and entire family and girlfriend down. He would listen to this famed aunt he had heard about for years.

"Do you own timeshare yourself, Owen?" asked the beautiful red- and silver-haired Mary Elizabeth, after sipping her customary solitary glass of Bulleit Frontier Straight Bourbon Whiskey imported from the gauche, southern U.S.

"Um, ah, er. No, I don't. I never really thought to own timeshare, to tell you the truth."

"Well, first, am I to thank you for telling the truth, and can I expect more of it?" deadpanned the emerging mentor to the slouching Owen Funkhauzer.

Once again, "Um, ah, er."

"Now let's get right to it, Owen. If you don't have a burn for the value of your product—whether you're selling timeshare, vacuum cleaners, derivative contracts, or democracy—then get the hell out immediately."

Niece Marianne winced a bit (she, too, owned none) and hid in a sip of her altogether delicious chard.

"I am here to tell you," with a thump to the table, not unlike Pa's variety, "you have to believe in your product. This is a bit corny, but it's a good enough starting point for us. Do you know what the last four letters of the word 'enthusiasm' stand for?"

"Um, ah . . . "

"I am sold myself."

Owen looked like he was just struck in the face. He was gobsmacked. In all his years, he'd never even allowed the narrative to enter his consciousness that owning timeshare would be a good idea. Hell, he could just borrow the family jet and go rent a hotel anywhere. Until now. It was swim time.

"Buyers, whether they know it or not, are looking past your words. No, check that. They are looking and feeling in-between your words, to sense how you truly feel about the product you are selling. It's like jazz and blues music or any beautiful speech. It's the tension around the notes and words that gets people to move."

"I have a dream."

"Mr. Gorbachev, tear down this wall."

"Today, I consider myself the luckiest man alive . . . "

"Jesus just left Chicago, and he's bound for New Orleans."

Mary Elizabeth reeled off quotes and sang a riff or two with stunning elocution. She was sonorous, forceful, and the entire Parisian café began to take notice. It didn't hurt that she had an amazing set of legs, sculpted by years of breaking mustangs and Corolla wild horses on Piedmont ranches and the North Carolina Outer Banks. She was her mother's daughter, too. Muscles on the top of her thigh poured proportionately over the muscles on the bottom half, creating a line of enchantment. That line extended right down through hardened calf muscles. Sheer beauty and power. A different kind

of beauty, mused Owen, than legs sculpted for muscu-
lature's sake in a gym. Muscles from ranch work were
better looking.

"Now, we all know charlatans can dupe folks in the
short term, to big gains. But eventually, it wears off."

Owen, for the first time in his life, felt a bit of fire
in his belly. Positive fire. Maybe the beginning of something he had unwittingly craved all his young, immature
life: a calling. Marianne, becoming proud of her intro-
duction, playfully reminded her boyfriend that she was
named for the French goddess of liberation.

Owen responded, "Yeah, I suppose that's why there
is a whole cottage industry for attorneys to get owners
out of timeshare products. People are figuring out they
might have been duped." Owen couldn't believe what
he had just said. Would a thunderbolt appear from
Grandpa Funk, or his sister, on his walk back to his flat?

The table went silent. And Mary Elizabeth was fine
and allowed for that. The patient was taking his medi-
cine.

"We three will meet again, after you two are owners
of the product you tout." She knocked back the whiskey with a swift, graceful maneuver and began to leave.
Long legs, in full stride, with purpose. She loved deliver-

ing a great exit—such a lost art. "Oh, and you'll pay full price, just like your customers."

Marianne was purchasing the timeshare package on her smartphone, via a delighted phone rep. The deal was done in minutes—off to the Seychelles the couple would go.

CHAPTER 9

God Rest Pa's Soul

It was a magical four nights for the young couple. They owned time for the first time. The process had precipitated an incalculably valuable discussion that would set the trajectory of their relationship. Owen got a vision to propose. While scuba diving, he started to know he wanted to spend the rest of his life with this incredible woman. They talked about a future, about a vision for a family. What?! Owen couldn't believe what was coming out of his mouth. But this vacation, this interruption from the blasted hurry of everyday life, was catalyzing deep meaning. And to think that since they owned in the Seychelles forever, this would continue forever. And it was theirs, not a hotel's. It was the most romantic experience of the young couple's life.

Owning your vacation could make sense.
Exciting sense. Is this what Grandpa Funk
envisioned originally?

Owen suddenly couldn't wait for their next visit with Mary Elizabeth.

The mentor had required several readings for the trip: ***Getting to Yes***, by Roger Fisher and William Ury; ***The Speed of Trust***, by Stephen M. R. Covey; ***The Power of Full Engagement***, by Jim Loehr and Tony Schwartz; ***Man's Search for Meaning***, by Viktor E. Frankl; and **"Storytelling That Moves People,"** an article about screenwriting coach Robert McKee.

Owen Funkhauzer had become so informed and inspired by his mentor, Mary Elizabeth Tabachnikov, that he would be a student of genuine persuasion, moments of meaning-making (MOMM), and purity of purpose, forever. A lifelong learner of among the most important art forms in which all souls ought to partake: authentic salesmanship.

Mary was hoping for the best for her student and his gal on their vacation. She meditated with high reverence, "God rest Pa's sweet soul."

CHAPTER 10

MOMM

The next meeting was different than the get-to-gether in the café. It was all business, in a hotel, with a conference room that had no windows.

Mary was ready to work and lay out her curriculum, MOMM – *Moments of Meaning-Making*. She was ready to transform her student, and hopefully, with luck and providence, an industry that desperately needed repair.

Her opus commenced.

"MOMM is about sincerity and surprise, Owen," as she gazed for emphasis. "You now believe in your product, know its every nook and cranny, and that's 100 percent of the deal. Here's the other 100 percent:

You must routinely go beyond the business
at hand with your tribe, to make meaning
with individual members.

45

"Your product has become commoditized. Robots can and do sell it. Your extended focus, going forward, will be on satisfying the client's unstated need. To actually lead him or her. Literally and existentially, you will take your clients to places they've never been. I've looked at that Fontaigne 5D, and it gives me a perfect blend of nausea and the hives. Your modus operandi, now that you are an owner and can speak sincerely about your product, is 180 degrees the opposite direction. Here is your MOMM 5D Counter-Offensive that will ultimately make you the winner of this contest and silence the lambs, including your misguided, cartoonish nemesis, Nick Fontaigne.

"Deliver:

1. Operational excellence with your product. It must perform.

2. Moments of meaning-making after each and every business engagement

3. Discipline to your prospects. Sometimes 'No' is the right thing. The Takeaway is foul and verboten.

4. Joy to all in your ecosystem

5. Continued contact with your flock, exchanging ideas

"Let's take each, one at a time, Owen and Marianne. I want you crystal clear on this approach."

For the first time in Owen's otherwise pathetic life of entitlement and physical comfort, he was sensing a feeling of power inside him. He couldn't describe in words, but there was a formation of substantial energy bubbling up from his inner core. It delighted him and scared him at once. Something was happening. The moment was beckoning.

The She-Master continued, "COMMODITY. Say it aloud with me. Timeshare can be gotten anywhere! Your product is like a gallon of milk or gasoline. How are you going to set yourself apart in a business race to the bottom?" Mary Elizabeth then ran a clip of Warren Buffet preaching to young businesspeople about the critical necessity of creating and retaining an extraordinary client experience. The Sage of Omaha talked up how a rental car company and furniture maker were dominating because of an earnest resolve to delight clients. "Did you hear the man? MOMM is the answer. MOMM is the disruption. Let's define it: *MOMM is a creative, compelling, and emotionally enthralling gesture that exceeds norms, and is readily retold as story.* It is your future.

"Here's how you do it:

"Every single engagement with a prospect or client or influential businessperson brings about the magic ingredient of MOMM: Information. I want you listening with ferocity, going beyond stated positions by the person, and hearing—and feeling—their interests. Their passion, interests, and pain points. I once told a business partner of mine, a guy who, too, had lost his dad recently, how much I appreciated the photograph of a bear he had taken, which was hanging in his office. How the bear actually resembled my late Russian-American father. Well, sure enough, four days later that photograph showed up framed as a creative gesture, along with a handwritten note about the joy of having a dad. Do you think I am going to find ways to help my business partner, after that extraordinary, thoughtful gesture?

"The key?

"*Information, interpersonal creativity, and action!* IIA is your way, if you care for goofy acronyms. Also, be mindful of your clients' personality types. I have a friend who's a hedge fund manager, a real driver. He answers the phone by saying, 'What?' Be bold, brief, brilliant, and be gone—with these types.

"You'll also run across socials—talk about the cat, the grandchild, the sports team, and be sincere. Socials need personal attention. Lastly, note the analytic personality.

Be accurate with everything you say. Have details locked down on pricing and terms. If not, you'll be dismissed!

"Any questions so far, you two?"

Owen felt like he was doing a gainer off a diving board. This was revolutionary stuff, entirely upending the manipulative blather he'd been taught forever in business development corporate seminars. He remembered the vile YouTube clip of "Always Be Closing" nonsense, delivered by Alec Baldwin in *Glengarry Glen Ross*. Amusing, but wretched, and ultimately a destructive approach, he reflected. He started to get clarity on the altogether terrible training in sales over the years. He began to see that the people doing the training were often incompetent at doing the selling themselves. They were political survival artists in their corporate cocoons. This person, Mary Elizabeth, was different. Really different.

Marianne's pretty face showed hope. "Go on, please."

"You also want to be sifting for clues as to how your clients appreciate being appreciated. What matters, with respect to emotional dynamics?" Mary points to Chapman's book on love languages. "Does your client appreciate being acknowledged? Or spending time with you? Or acts of service? *Pay attention; here lie the keys to a lifetime client!* And every move you make is in the spirit of genuine, full-disclosure, Sunshine! You are relentlessly looking for ways to connect emotionally, like no other, and contribute value. Forget achievement in your careers; think contribution and purity of purpose. All of what I am saying constitutes MOMM—you live it now. And heck, it all comes back to MOMM, anyway.

"Furthermore, you must win a sense of the communication preference of your potential clients. *How do they want to receive information from you?* For example, that hard-charging driver might want a text at 6 a.m. with the pricing information he had requested. Because down deep, he wants to see you're up and working at the crack of dawn, too. Also, back to the future: Bring back the handwritten note! Does anybody on Planet Earth want to receive another email or text today? NO. Alternatively, everyone appreciated deeply a thoughtful, sincere, handwritten note. The documents you write, when done with sincerity and surprise, will sit on the desks of your flock for very long periods of time. They're guaranteed meaning-makers! Just include a graph for your analytic types!

"Next, for your flock, you want to think in terms of perpetuity. Delivering for MOMM, meaning-making, in a habituated manner. Appoint a team member, someone with high emotional intelligence, which means they comprehend interpersonal creativity naturally, seamlessly, as your Chief Experience Officer. Empower that individual. Have weekly meetings as to how you may expand your capacity for meaning-making; that's where the best ideas for interpersonal impact will emerge. Bonnie Raitt sings, 'Let's give them something to talk about.' Do that!

"Next, you two must light a fire for the purpose of getting all engaged with MOMM. When teams come alive with this concept, enduring results cannot help but follow for the enterprise. Here is a turnkey process for catalyzing MOMM in your team practice.

1. Live it thyself. Your team will listen to MOMM, and inherently they will feel her ringing true. But if the culture is not genuinely signaling that the initiative is for real, entropy will happen, creeping in and precipitating mediocre interpersonal engagement, like a wet blanket. As a leader, you must live it yourself, demonstrating creative gestures to each other in appropriate and thoughtful intervals. As such, do you know what animates your teammates? What are their greatest passions and pain points? Why are they working in your organization, beyond remuneration? As

a leader, how can you expand your capacity for meaning-making with your troops? You must be appropriate with MOMM; going over the top, or generating what feels like a contrived atmosphere, will only disappoint. The key for hitting the mark for MOMM is regular discussions with other leadership; there's where you'll find the best ideas emerging, subtly, as soft as sunrises. Or sometimes, like a thunderbolt.

2. Ask this question at the start of every team meeting: *Who or what is getting this team's best energy and are we okay with this?* The question allows MOMM to go to work, keeping her on an appropriate course. You'll find it stunning how easy it is to fall off the mark, to get muddled in the everyday humdrum busyness of life. The question is like a swift jab to the head, a rebuke to the bland of existence, and keeps your team focused and energized in the right direction.

3. As the expression goes, if you want to go somewhere quickly, go alone. If you want to go somewhere great, go with a committed team and MOMM. Jeff Bezos says a key to great leadership is being like a broken record. To your team you must say, over and over and over, the value of

delivering for MOMM. And to your team you must model, over and over and over, MOMM.

4. Hold yourself accountable for creating and delivering an environment where team creativity can flourish. Remember, in a commoditized world, it's a flat-out race for the best ideas to make meaning with clients. And nothing squashes MOMM's magic more than undue emotional and mental team stress. Interpersonal creativity cannot, and will not, come to be when a dark energy appears in the culture. Are you ensuring the work pace is sensible in your organization? Do you insist on and celebrate the utmost critical need for proper work breaks and vacations? Do you insist and celebrate outstanding tenacity that has been exhibited on behalf of clients or potential clients? This is radical, anti-5D, incidentally, and the approach always wins out, over time, with proper tending. Consider this story on outstanding interpersonal creativity. A client I am coaching told of the time he arrived at the Chicago Ritz-Carlton with his wife and two daughters, ages 7 and 9. They were there for the weekend to enjoy the Celine Dion concert. As they exited the vehicle on a Thursday,

one of the daughters mumbled jubilantly about her excitement for the concert on Saturday to a MOMM-devotee bellman: 'Two whole days away!' Well, come Saturday afternoon at around 3:00, a different bellman came to their door with this to say: 'I hope you are all enjoying your stay. Say, I know how excited you are about the Celine Dion concert tonight. She is actually warming up right now on the piano downstairs here at the hotel. I asked her if it would be okay for you four to join her as she warms up, and she said, "Sure."' Now, that's MOMM, folks—what disruptive thoughtfulness. Do you think that family will ever stop telling that story? And every time they do, they burnish the reputation of the iconic hotel.

5. With teamwork for MOMM, trust is ingredient numero uno. When trust goes up, the amount of work for MOMM skyrockets. It's axiomatic. The question I have for you and your team is, 'How do you create more of the gold? Of trust?' Here's part of the answer: Your teammates want to get glimpses of the real, vulnerable you. Show 'em. Tell 'em. But again, a key word for MOMM will always lurk: appropriateness. Nobody wants

a leader bumbling and groveling on about his or her weaknesses and disappointments. No, that gets pathetic. A groveling leader is of no value. But a transformative leader is going to give you glimpses of what is really animating him or her. Flashes of pain points, that are buttressed with vignettes of strength and a plan for the future.

"One cannot take five steps in this timeshare industry without hearing the word 'disruption.' So, let's go with it for your planning on your leadership going forward. Let's disrupt how you communicate. Let's send Power-Point decks to the trash heap of rhetorical history.

"Why is it that presenters in timeshare feel compelled to use excessive verbiage on slides? How many times in your career have you felt deluged with info on fees, swapping options, or 'How do I get to Paris over Christmas'? The norm is excessive verbiage. A participant in your audience, say a prospect or sales associate, has three options when one of those dizzying slides makes its appearance in their view:

1. Read the slide.

2. Listen to the presenter.

3. Abort engagement altogether, and ponder their child's chances in her forthcoming soccer match.

"All too often, and this will come as no surprise, they choose option C, with some slight modification to the actual daydream. In fact, researchers at the Human Performance Institute instruct that in today's hyper-frenetic world, folks are listening to about 30 percent of the presenter's content. About 35 percent of your client's or prospect's precious mental engagement is dithering to matters of their future; the balance, to matters of their past.

"You will stop. You will disrupt.

"For compliance and other reasons, I fully recognize the need for your sales teams to use decks with which to circulate and socialize, internally and externally, on whatever it is the presenter will be discussing. But when the rubber hits the road, and you are actually presenting in front of people who represent revenue to your enterprise, to throw up a slide with excessive verbiage is suicide. Again, the listener often aborts engagement, neither listening nor reading the bullets. This is not just according to me per se, but to Steve Jobs and a researcher who published 'Death by PowerPoint.' Can you relate to the feeling of being killed by a PowerPoint presentation? I have yet to meet a player in our industry who cannot.

"As long as we presenters are aware of the occasional 'need' for some extra verbiage, due again, usually to compliance, we can tiptoe with tactics of efficacy. Here's what you will do:

- Simply turn the screen off when presenting for extended periods, then return to it.

- Replace stats with stories.

- Replace verbiage with images.

- Consider becoming a master of your topic and simply hand out a copy of the slides after your presentation.

"Further, an ex-lover of mine and industry consultant, Mark Magnacca, is adamant of the need for presenters to hammer home the 'So What?' of the message. Who cares, and why should anyone be listening? Learning theory for adults (andragogy) suggests quite clearly that business executives need to know, and be retold several times, *why* they are learning *what* they are learning. Moreover, according to change specialist Jon Kotter, there must be a clear sense of urgency with what is being requested of the audience to do, as a result of the speech.

"Follow these guidelines on public speaking, you two. It's how you'll stand out against the parade of platitudinous presenters. Are we clear?"

"Yup." Holy cow, what a speech; wish I had heard this years ago, the couple thought.

"Lastly," said Mary, driving the point home, "Here is where nuclear business growth happens. Know this: The future of your business is in the imaginations of your happy clients. They *can* and *will* grow your business with tremendous velocity. The key? Humility. Asking for their advice—NEVER FOR A REFERRAL—on how to grow your club with other members just like them. *The advice of the wise is like a life-giving fountain.* Ask for advice on how to grow your business, and you will experience exponential growth in business like you've never seen before. Here is where you can expect to crush the 5D process of interpersonal pollution."

If an individual could experience the paradox of being energized and dumbfounded at the same time, it would be Owen and Marianne, at that moment. Revolutionary counsel has that effect.

CHAPTER 11

An Inkling

Big Daddy Funk was prepping for his semiannual board meeting in familiar form. Resting—like a lion. Gathering energy and knowledge to unload on his board members. Earlier in his career he had stumbled upon a scientific study that had changed his life. *Personal energy is the asset of primacy; managing the asset of time is secondary.* It was simplicity shock, among the most logical and profound bits of knowledge he had ever procured. The key to doing so, of creating more and higher-quality energy? A fancy, $3 word said it all: Oscillation, which means non-correlating work rituals that will let the mind and emotions regenerate. Only few knew that Funk, like his hero, Winston Churchill, was an outstanding painter. He felt his work mind strengthen as his artistic mind danced on the canvas, every single day. There would be zero interruptions during Funk's painting time.

Further, in preparation, Funk had gathered and was assessing data about the emotional state of his audience. He went through a thought process set on catalyzing his physical, mental, and emotional reservoirs. He knew he needed all three for full impact, to draw the desired effect with his board: increased firm spending on promotions and training of the 5D process. Clearly, Funk had concluded, Nick was going to win, destroying his grandson in the contest, five months in.

Yet, as Funk sipped another club soda and munched on some almonds, a dim, darker feeling—thorn-like—was setting in on him, as if this preparation for combat was lacking for something. In completely uncharacteristic form, he actually glanced at an email from an altogether relentless vendor. Funk opened the message, "Here's the Sauce, From Thommy Fross," and reflected deeply:

> *The two most important days of your life are*
> *the day you were born and the day you find*
> *out why.* – MARK TWAIN

That night, exhausted from a great talk and engaging follow-up Q&A, Funk dreamt with brilliant clarity. A phantasmagoria of colors, conversations, and songs, better than the best sales meeting he had ever assembled. A visage then appeared, at once awe-inspiring and serene. It was a peculiar amalgam of Big Papi, from the Boston Red Sox, and Charlton Heston. The question emerged with a force and radiance, and South Boston accent for good measure: "I gave you life, and what did you do with it?"

Funk awoke—with extraordinary energy and heightened purpose.

CHAPTER 12

It's a Horror Show

Mary Elizabeth came back from the break more focused than ever. Marianne and Nick were taken aback at her pugnacity.

"Let's get something straight right now. You will not use The Takeaway in any shape or form. It is manipulation and a horror show. And here's the thing; whenever a takeaway is executed 'successfully,' it will always, always, eventually come undone. The client will eventually get the sense that he or she was duped. Then, do you know what sets in?

RESENTMENT.

"The worst of human emotions 'cause it's so hard to undo. When you determine that you have been hornswoggled into buying a product, deep-seated anger understand-ably sows. Over time, the emotion burgeons and calcifies. An eventual resentment has to manifest, and then it putrefies the brand called 'you.'

"Your team, Owen, will therefore conduct itself in the opposite, high-grounded manner. You will insist, as probity will orchestrate, to NOT sell your products to inappropriate buyers. If the finances are not in place, you will not sell. If the potential client does not understand the product, you will not sell. Do you understand? Teshuvah! *(Owen would google this last term at break: 'proper conduct,' in Hebrew.)*

"You will sign the following oath, or I discontinue my consulting at this very moment:

> *I will never sell anything to anyone*
> *who does not need it."*

Owen was back doing a gainer off the diving board. Talk about unconventional. Are you kidding? Is this woman mad? Would Grandpa Funk be okay with this? What would investors of the firm conclude from this business development creed?

Mary then declared she would read a poem by Michael Josephson, "*What Will Matter.*"

Ready or not, some day it will all come to an end.
There will be no more sunrises,

no minutes, hours or days.
All the things you collected,
whether treasured or forgotten
will pass to someone else.
Your wealth, fame and temporal power
will shrivel to irrelevance.
It will not matter what you owned
or what you were owed.
Your grudges, resentments, frustrations
and jealousies will finally disappear.

So too, your hopes, ambitions, plans
and to-do lists will expire.
The wins and losses that once seemed
so important will fade away.
It won't matter where you came from
or what side of the tracks you lived on at the end.
It won't matter whether you were beautiful or brilliant.
Even your gender and skin color will be irrelevant.

So what will matter?
How will the value of your days be measured?

What will matter is not what you bought
but what you built, not what you got
but what you gave.
What will matter is not your success
but your significance.

What will matter is not what you learned
but what you taught.
What will matter is every act of integrity,
compassion, courage, or sacrifice
that enriched, empowered or encouraged others
to emulate your example.

What will matter is not your competence
but your character.
What will matter is not how many people you knew,
but how many will feel a lasting loss when you're gone.
What will matter is not your memories
but the memories that live in those who loved you.
What will matter is how long you will be remembered,
by whom and for what.

Living a life that matters doesn't happen by accident.
It's not a matter of circumstance but of choice.
Choose to live a life that matters.

Owen's and Marianne's jaws dropped. This was a different way of going about business development, to say the least. The conventional wisdom of sales training, with a cigarette hanging from its mouth and a 5D training brochure, had been jettisoned headlong out of the window by MOMM, bad cologne and all.

Only one thing to do now—see if Mary Elizabeth's way worked.

For some inexplicable reason, Marianne quietly felt a sense of relief from the otherwise agonizing dread of the lawsuits that had come her company's way in the last several years. Resentment manifest, indeed.

CHAPTER 13

Groovin'

Meanwhile, back at the showroom floor in Shanghai, Fontaigne's team was on fire. Inspired by his hero, professional wrestler Slick Ric Flair, Nick would send short messages to his sales "studs," as he'd like to address them. They were sometimes fictitious in nature, like Rocko:

"My name is Rocko G. Vaselini, and the G stands for Groovin'." Or, "Lubbock, Texas, my kind of town, because I own half of it." He then emitted a brief sound of his golden dog howling.

The sales studs, men and women alike, were worked up into an almost lather. They were making money. China and Pan-Asia were gulping down the concept of vacation ownership. The 5D process, which required only small adjustments for the cultural differences, was proving itself in spades. People just could not bear the thought of missing out on the timeshare craze. Momentum was substantial, and The Hell Yeah cannon was doing its thing routinely. Eight months into it, and there were no signs of resentment.

Yet.

Then one day, Xi Chung walked his family into the showroom to hear a pitch so he and his family could "earn" some gaming chips for the blackjack table.

He was a grand man, winsome in nature, long on intellect, and a physical specimen who retained a standing challenge to any of his 22 grandchildren in a pull-up competition. He could recite a quote from Mencius, Cicero, or King Solomon with overwhelming and appropriate zeal. Nobody laughed as hard as he. Libo Zhou, Jim Carrey, and the Three Stooges (Curly being the choicest, due to girth) were among his favorite comedians, yielding guffaws that unleashed a mighty belly. Yet, in turn, he could be as serious and as solemn as a Taoist monk, reciting stories of the Qing dynasty, preaching forbearance or sincerity to rapt offspring. There were only two kinds of art in the world: good and bad. *One Hundred Horses* by Lang Shining was the former; *Crazy Rich Asians*, very much the latter. So much so, he needed extra turmeric to settle his grand stomach after viewing. He loved his country and family as much as any patriarch. He was as fine a Chinese man, or human being, as any.

The Takeaway worked swimmingly with Xi, always believing the best in folks and not wanting to miss out on a trend. He bought three Premium Deluxe packages for his family. What Fontaigne, taking the bigger opportunity himself, didn't realize at the time of executing his 5D, was that the Chung family held vast influential prestige, beyond Fontaigne's scope of comprehension.

A tat printed on the heel of each Chung family member read, *chaoji daguo*. They would give their lives for Chinese nationality.

Trouble was, one of Xi's sons was not as steeped in virtue as his iconic father.

CHAPTER 14

Angels Singing

Owen sat down with Olivia Hails in his first presentation since the deep-dive training with Mary Elizabeth. He could not believe how comfortable he felt. He started to tell his story, sincerely and wholeheartedly, about the Seychelles. Would this actually work? Intermittently, he looked for signals from Olivia. What was going on with her . . . really? Her interests? Pain points? How could he satisfy an unstated, or even unrecognized, need? Owen harkened back to a portion of Mary's lecture on going past the golden and platinum rules. The golden rule requires the treatment of others the way you yourself would want to be treated. Beyond that, the platinum rule requires the treatment of others the way *they* would want to be treated. Mary's way, the supreme flow between rabbi and student, was that of titanium: Treat others the way they *need* to be treated. In other words, lead.

As the conversation moved on—and it was brisk because the potential buyer was a driver—with Owen sharing some limitations of his product with as much candor as the preponderant merits, Olivia began to speak about the difficulties she was having with her 20-year-old daughter. That she had not been able to connect meaningfully with her ever since the death of her horse, Mr. Tibbs, an American Paint. Owen, hearing Mary Elizabeth in his head, began to probe gently. The only thing that seemed to energize the daughter was horseback riding. Owen then asserted. He went right to an ownership property that specialized in everything equestrian in Idaho. "Do you think your daughter might appreciate being an owner of this forever?"

Silence.

Then a teardrop from Olivia.

When the paperwork was complete, Owen executed his commitment to Mary—and went one step further. He sent the daughter a classic portrait of a Paint, with a handwritten note: "May you find your next Mr. Tibbs in Idaho."

Two weeks later, Owen received a text from Olivia: "Just had the best conversation with my daughter in 10 years. WOW. Angels are singing, Owen! And I want you to talk to my cousin about buying with us in Idaho too. I'll text you her contact info."

Oh, baby, it's on, thought Owen Funkhauzer. He had never felt such a lightning bolt in his entire life. He noticed a slight change in his gait. He stood higher and felt he was taking up more space, in a grander way, like an oak tree that had just made an advance upward to precious sunshine. He was finding his way.

CHAPTER 15

Longhorn Shot Glass, Airborne

On the second morning of month 14 of the contest, Nick would receive an email that would promptly ruin his day. And his colleagues at the office were about to get quite a sonorous surprise.

There it was. The cold number in an antiseptic spreadsheet. Owen's sales run was higher than Nick's. There had been a trend in the last number of weeks of Owen's surge. Nick dismissed it as luck, or perhaps as a result from sly referrals from Grandpa. But this was the tipping point when reality could not be escaped.

Nick had sold a barrage of weeks to a prominent Texas natural gas family by phone from China. Old Lady Winthrop was so delighted with being part of Nick's club, she had sent him a shot glass with a University of Texas Longhorn emblem. It was thick and heavy.

Nick had once thrown a baseball 90 mph in his younger years.

The sound of a shot glass zooming through an office at 85 mph makes a brief but piercing hiss, as if sipping in air brusquely with your teeth. When the shot glass traveling 85 mph strikes a glass mirror, it makes an altogether grandiloquent cacophony. Nick had spotted his image in that mirror, and with the information about his new place in the sales contest now available for the whole firm to peruse on their handheld devices, rage ensued. Big Texas rage.

Sales associates and marketing managers sat motionless in the area as glass slowly kept sprinkling to the floor, tens of seconds after the burst.

Razzmatazz tucked his nub of a tail down low, crouched a bit, and sauntered into his supersized pen, The Alamo. All was not well in Shanghai, and things would be getting much worse for Nick "I Make Rain" Fontaigne.

CHAPTER 16

Chung Suffers No Fools

Mr. Chung initially had loved the idea of timeshare ownership. He was a proud man, with his family hailing back to a great Chinese dynasty. His businesses were thriving around the region, and he had big plans to expand. He was even considering hiring Nick to come lead training on the 5D to his business development managers.

But then the problem happened.

Mr. Chung needed to make a change on the week he owned to attend a graduation for his nephew. He was unable. He thought he would be able. The nice phone assistant for the firm, operating out of India, was accustomed to dealing with frustrated customers. Not a worry. But this call seemed different. There was a force of discontent on the other end of the line, the likes of which she had not experienced. A deep tone emerged

79

from the consternation of the client. An accomplished patriarch had been scorned.

Mr. Chung did not suffer fools well, especially not when the leader—now the latest adversary—was an overbearing American, wearing too much cologne. Fontaigne would promptly be given the unceremonious nickname by the Xi family of "General Tso Chicken," which, like the windbag timeshare charlatan, was an American phony that had no roots in the great Chinese culture.

CHAPTER 17

Vital, and Incidental

Grandpa Funk's existential puzzle was becoming solved. Over all these years he had thought about what he would bring to bear in business. He was constantly checking in on his emotional, mental, and physical dimensions as a person. He was fit as a fiddle and mentally alert, recalling names, facts, and figures like a walking algorithm. Emotionally he was charged, but balanced. Yet when he was briefed on the new, compelling curriculum his grandson was bringing to bear for his firm, it dawned on him:

The aim in his business would be meaning-making for clients from this day forward.

This profundity would round out his approach to his otherwise incomplete modus operandi. Here lay the fourth and culminating piece to his puzzle: the spiritual dimension. Somehow, he was given the gift to form a spectacular global firm, and the gift of moving on, after his granddaughter's death. Likewise, he now was committed to giving gifts to his clients. Not free product; the business mattered. But this woman, Mary Elizabeth, in her personal podcast for Owen's team, was right on the money, and completed him. He would bring sunshine to every client he could, going beyond the business at hand.

He felt lightness and warmth. He knew, now, why he was born. His firm, though vital to his supreme mission, suddenly felt incidental. *Vital, and incidental*—he would have the paradox subtly engraved on the granite in his office suite. A reminder, here forward, for which this firm would stand.

CHAPTER 18

"You Don't Know What the Hell You're Missing"

Nick Fontaigne couldn't believe his own eyes, that he was tampering with the secret sauce of his 5D Interpersonal Rock-the-World Process. How could that privileged dork from HR possibly be able to do this to him and his dream of familial regentrification?

Something had to give.

There had been no fluke. Owen's team in Europe was moving forward each month now, walloping Nick's team. Short video clips were being recorded of individual MOMM gestures by sales associates and shared throughout the firm, to inspire and teach the curriculum. Results were amassing, without the dreaded high rescission rates of deals that 5D created. Good heavens! Intellectual disruption giants like Salim Ismail of the famed Singularity University called, requesting an exclusive interview as to how Owen was creating such exponential growth.

SALIM: Forgive me, sir, but just what the heck is going on in your business unit that is creating such astonishing growth in an industry that would otherwise appear to be mature and perhaps complete in any momentum formation?

OWEN: MOMM is the answer.

SALIM: I beg your pardon.

OWEN: It always comes back to MOMM anyway *(with smile)*. Our approach is an interpersonal disruption mechanism, where sincerity and interpersonal creativity lie at the center. We have jettisoned standard, typical, manipulative sales training techniques and have elected to traverse an unconventional path.

Owen, for the first time in his life, was speaking with an attribute entirely alien to him heretofore:

CONVICTION.

SALIM *(with a mutter)*: Conviction convinces, doesn't it, Owen?

OWEN: Conviction disrupts, Salim.

Industry bloggers were now regularly contacting Owen, not Nick, for interviews.

One blog title created a particularly acute sense of Texas-red ire: "The Privileged Kid Takes Away the Texas Street Dog's Lead in Timeshare Sales Contest."

Well, here would come the rage again. And the thing about uncontrolled rage—it usually leads to action. Regrettable action. Like having to write one heck of a check to replace a mirror.

Or to the consequences of hiring Mutsuhiro Watanabe. Mutsuhiro was a toughness trainer, and the only surviving Japanese kamikaze fighter pilot of WWII. He had one leg. And he wanted to add an extra D to the curriculum—"Damn it!"

Mutsuhiro believed Nick's team had gotten soft. There needed to be greater intensity of delivery of the 5D. Takeaways should be deployed with outright ferocity, not passive aggression. For example, "You don't know what the hell you're missing!" as opposed to, "This club is not for everyone."

Nick was reluctant at first, but becoming desperate. He had even challenged Owen to a YouTube-produced cage fight. Owen declined, though Mary Elizabeth enjoyed reading the advanced email offer, over a sip of Kentucky Red.

Nick called an emergency meeting for his team. All sales associates were to be assembled for two days of intense training, of 5D augmentation, in a remote province within sight of the Great Wall. Mutsuhiro would have complete command of the 20-hour training. Diets were restricted. All handheld devices were to be handed over to Mutsuhiro's assistants. Restroom breaks were only allotted at Mutsuhiro's command, and there would be four minutes to execute discharge.

Halfway through the training, Nick felt nauseous. He could barely compete in the group exercise. For team chemistry formation, Mutsuhiro had ordered a game of Fire in the Hole on the impeccable lawn outside the hotel. Just after nightfall, teams of seven associates would each take the 11 squares of toilet paper issued by Mutsuhiro and insert one end into his or her hindquarters. With a tail hanging down from the naked individual, Mutsuhiro would then light the bottom of each of the bumwad strings. The associate would then run as far as they could, creating quite a spectacle, with his six colleagues, all with fannies ablaze. Whenever a "baby sun of inspiration" *(Japanese language)* would disappear into a backside, the ongoing spectators/hecklers would exhort "Fire in the hole!" at the top of their lungs. Whoever went the furthest, with fanny ablaze, won. A commissioned DJ would then play Jimi Hendrix's "Let Me Stand Next to Your Fire." It was a hoot.

Nick played only half-heartedly, and glumly read on his handheld the rebuke from HR about the inappropriateness of vendor Mutsuhiro's Fire in the Hole game. He had never received negative memos from HR before. An inkling emerged that the training would do no good.

He was right. Results eight weeks later only accelerated the beating Nick was taking. A takeaway without nuance, without slippery linguistic manipulation, misses marks. And worse still, the blitzkrieg takeaway, as Mutsuhiro liked to borrow language from his Second World War ally, did damage. It created an immediate Anti-MOMM, which, like a MOMM, turned into a story that would pass through the constituency of clients.

Mutsuhiro was expediting the toxicity of Nick's brand.

CHAPTER 19

Defend Richmond

Fontaigne was mulling over Confederate battles, looking for where mistakes had been made in the greatest of all engagements, the Civil War, and trying to learn. He was past his mistake with Mutsuhiro. Though dog-faced and desultory, he kept pouring over internet blogs by Southern history professors. What came up with regular frequency was how Gen. Robert E. Lee, the culminating hero to the timeshare salesman charlatan, spent too much time and too many resources defending Richmond, the capital of the Southern Confederacy. Defending, defending, defending. You don't win by defending. You win by asserting. With a canine mystique, Razzmatazz stirred with excitement, golden hairs standing erect behind his massive head. His master was coming upon a strategic adjustment; victory would return.

Fontaigne concluded he had been reduced to too much defending of late. Defending his 5D strategy, his Richmond. No, sir, it was time for a change, as he threw back another slog of anti-hangover supplementation and scratched his rear end.

He referred to the most important operating document of his career: The 48 Laws of Power. When his mind was clear, he could recite from memory all 48 commands. An opus of stunning Machiavelli proportion and likeness, the document focused on full domination of the opponent. Of getting what you wanted at all costs. The book rested like gunpowder on Fontaigne's dresser in his study, right next to the photograph of a great white shark, fully breached from the Mediterranean Sea, instilling his ferocious bite into a seal, named "grandson," with a Sharpie pen.

Laws 14, 25, 32, and 38 leapt off the page at him.

Pose as a friend; work as a spy. Oh, yes, of course. The dim-witted nose-picker son of the founder got lucky. Bumped into a selling process that was kind of good, maybe. Time to pick up the phone and be a friend to the little twit.

"You guys have done well over there in France. Good for you, pal! I am proud of you."

A reluctant Owen stayed with the conversation. He couldn't believe his ears, and actually started to appreciate the phone call. He liked to please, after all.

"Thanks, Nick. So awesome of you to call. I am so proud of my team, but you know, I got to give you thanks for lighting the fire. I was lost till you and the 5D got us rolling! How's Razzmatazz doing, by the way?"

"I appreciate you asking. The varmint is getting ready to do some breeding for me. I might get him with a pretty Rottweiler and see what we could create. You interested in a pup?"

The fawning Funkhauzer was flattered. He couldn't even bear lending thought to what an oversized, obnoxious Great Dane and a Rotty might yield.

"Sounds great, Nick. Put me down for one pup! I will call him or her Freddy 5."

"My arse, you will," thought Fontaigne, about to get sick from this conversation. But he gently strolled his primary index finger over the treasured copy of *The 48 Laws of Power*, and proceeded to the plan.

"You got it, partner. You'll get the pick of the litter. Say, can you help your old pal out? Give Daddy a little taste of what this MOMM dang thing is all about. I mean, you know, don't give your secret sauce, 'cause we still got a nice competition cooking. But a little insight would be groovy."

Owen was still so naive. He was just too tickled that this former bully was paying him such heed. Such apparent warmth. Heck, maybe someday they could work together for the goodness of Grandpa's incredible company.

"I'll tell you, Nick. The real trick with your team is a bit of a paradox."

"Paradox? What do a pair of cocks have anything to do with this?" deadpanned Nick, as he picked his ear and stared at the ceiling.

"Ha ha, ha ha," said Owen. "What I mean is, MOMM protocol must be inspired with the team; it cannot be required. The team has to buy in, to believe, in earnest, or else time just gets wasted."

"Wasted time? Right, Owen. I hear you. Thanks, man. Let's stay in touch through the finish line and beyond."

Nick promptly hit play on "Ain't Wastin' Time No More," by The Allman Brothers. Hell no, he wasn't wasting time no more, dismissing entirely the message just delivered by Owen. Time to steal MOMM. It was time, as Law 25 demanded, to recreate himself, in the spirit of resilience and total victory. It was time to pretend to deliver moments of meaning.

Ellen March, family matriarch, was thinking about buying timeshare in a lump sum for her considerable family that resided part-time in Utah and part-time in Beijing. Nick decided he would make his move to deliver what would appear as a creative gesture to Mrs. March, to help seal the deal. He wanted the bottle of Beau Joie Brut Champagne delivered right on time, in front of all the family members assembled at the handsome Grand America Hotel in downtown Salt Lake City. This would be tremendous; all in the wealthy family would then certainly learn who he was. And want more of his product.

The bottle arrived perfectly timed, smack-dab in front of 53 tall, blond, and blended Asian-American family members . . .

. . . who happened to be Mormon . . .

. . . and who never drank a lick of alcohol.

Oops, Ellen and fam. Anti-MOMM.

Anyway, proceed with the plan—defend Richmond. Defend your vested engagement in this sales contest.

So, look at Law 32, and play to people's fantasies, with an adapted version of MOMM. An ugly version, not that Nick Fontaigne believed there was any distinction.

He deployed an app that simulated handwritten notes and began sending out messages in a snowstorm-like frenzy. It was such a beautiful thing to Nick: Create the illusion that you were sitting down and earnestly taking the time and energy requisite to convey a handwritten note. But do it en masse, thanks to technology, supplicant to masquerades. Get the fruit without doing the real work. And above all, like Law 32 stipulated, play to people's fantasies. Make 'em each feel like a million bucks with platitudinous mass letters of inauthenticity. Oh, yes, fabulous. Stealing MOMM could be fun and useful.

Until the problem with spelling.

Cranking out letters with the app of meaning-making en masse one afternoon, Nick neglected to check in, to double-check his messaging. To his hundreds of centers of influence, who could drive the development of his business, he wrote:

"Remember, I can't wait to see you at my golf tournament on the sexth of October."

To 250 associates, clients, and potential clients, this "personalized, handwritten note" went out.

94

And just what do you think these influencers stumbled upon in their discussions with each other at the event? Fontaigne's handwritten notes were phony. And his error was downright hysterical; certainly worthy of countless tweets. "Sex in October with Nick Fontaigne—are we all getting screwed?" quipped one competing timeshare executive.

Ugly MOMM exacts her toll.

Nick's instincts told him to get back to the showroom floor. To Sell. To Hustle. But was the quality of the leads waning? Was the marketing department out to do him in by sending poorly qualified prospects? He finally lost his temper when Sally Fu, 101 years old, shuffled in to hear his presentation. It took her 2 1/2 minutes just to have a seat. Nick knew she was only there to gather the free gaming chips for the Shanghai Funky Dragon Casino later. He started in on his "Rent vs. Own Return on Investment" spiel with a hint of exasperation.

"Look Miss Sally, normally I run my rent vs. own analysis for future clients using 20 or 30 years. But in your case, let's just run it through next Tuesday."

Things were starting to unwind.

Nick tried to drown his sorrows back at The Wolf-pack Shanghai bar and grill. The inscription on his glass table read softly,

"He who rides the tiger cannot dismount."

Nick got the feeling he was riding the tiger of the 5D. He simply could not stop. This faking the MOMM was not panning out. It seems it could not pan out. Still, he returned to Law 38, in the sacred Laws of Power. *Think as you like, but behave like others.* Yes, brilliant. There's the adjustment that can make all the difference. Feigning familiarity.

With tremendous effort and resolve, Nick would dismount the tiger and change his comportment. He would behave like all other managers in the timeshare industry would behave. This would do the trick, as he continued to think differently, of strategizing to defend his 5D, or Richmond.

Things at the Shanghai HQ started to quiet a bit. The theatrics would soften. For sure, The Takeaway would still be left in place, working its magic, but now more subdued. More softly, more conventional, more laminated-like. He was behaving normatively, like the industry wanted him to behave. He rolled the cannon back into a warehouse. He restricted Razzmatazz from too much access. He would become humdrum.

Ultimately, Law 38 was of little utility. The sales numbers took no measurable move upward, and Nick's health began to careen from all the stress.

CHAPTER 20

Red Dot Above Kneecap

Nick was still hospitalized from the anxiety attacks that had come on suddenly. More consistently, he started to feel as if all the blood was oozing from his arms and legs, with fingers and toes tingling. Panic set in, though not a soul would be made aware of his situation. He was descending into rock bottom. He went 2 1/2 days with no sleep at one point. Trying harder and harder. Defending Richmond. All the work, all the planning and execution of the 5D, was coming undone, and the great Nick Fontaigne was coming unglued. He had a dim feeling, inexplicable but as real as rain, that he had been duped. That the narratives bounding around between his ears all these years were a sham. With a totality of exhaustion, shame made her debut to Fontaigne. Finding himself fully prostrate one afternoon, in complete despair, he glanced slowly to his right. There in pencil, thinly written on the inside cover of an unread copy of Dostoevsky's book, *The Idiot* (a gift from a concerned client), was his New Year's promise to give more resources, time, and energy to the Wounded Warriors Project—to the men and women keeping all free. He hadn't done one, solitary thing for the organization. Shame's noose tightened.

He could not attend the grand affair back at The Hut to conclude the sales contest. In his hospital room in southern Shanghai, he got up for a brief stroll and paused to gaze out of his window. Head hung low, he concluded, "What the hell have I done?" Then, in an instant, it appeared—a red dot just over his kneecap. The author of the red dot, with one eye shut and the other fully focused down a rifle sight line, softly muttered "Bok, bok, bok," in a nod to General Tso. This bullet was for the chicken. It took a moment, but Nick quickly deduced the horrific implications of the red dot and tried to jump backwards.

Too late.

The pain of the rifle shot was electric. The bullet was not unfamiliar to the surgeon, minutes later. Inscribed in tiny fashion on the bullet was "*CD*." It would be some time before the great Texas salesman would walk again.

Meanwhile, at The Hut, Funk would give the greatest speech of his life, before enjoying a delicious glass of bourbon with his newest and what would be greatest friendship of his life.

"For the majority of my career, I had it backwards. If I was to work hard—and I mean full-grit forward, whether shooting down Japanese Zeros in the Coral Sea *(the trainer winces)* or getting financed to start this glorious firm—then happiness and joy would come about some day *(with emphasis)*. I love this firm. I love you people. Even Nick, who we hope returns soon with that damn awful cannon, his big-balled varmint, and a new U.T. shot glass. But through pain and toil—heavens, I miss my granddaughter—and the Almighty tempering the wind to this shorn lamb, and with the help of so many others over the years, I was plain lucky to get a recent glimpse of truth. Sweet knowledge kind of bubbled up, like that gin-clear, 72-degree water at DeFuniak Springs just east of our hut here. Sweet glory *(pounding of table with full exposure of his power paws)*! This firm is vital, and incidental. The high aim from this time forward, The Imperative, is meaning-making with you and our beloved clients and partners. Purpose beyond self *(and his gaze settled in with force, but with deeply expanded compassion this time)*. We'll still get after it, mind you, and give those rascal competitors hell, but the aim has changed. It has elevated. Owen, I am so proud of you,

I could spit. You and Marianne brought the fountain of youth to this old Marine's bones. Now, will you all join me in a solitary slug of Kentucky bourbon?"

He continued by reciting Teddy Roosevelt's "The Man in the Arena," with an explicit nod to his dear grandson. He cried, just a little, with a remembrance of his granddaughter. The theme of "purpose beyond self" immediately went viral. Executives from countless industries began sharing the speech with their firms. Funk was transformed, which meant he was transforming others. Owen took in the speech with a tear in his eyes.

Marianne held his hand firmly and whispered into her fiancé's ear, "SVP."

The End

Discussion Topics for Business Development Teams

▶ What is the difference between Nick's WHY and Elliot's ultimate WHY? Is one about "Me" the other about "We"?

▶ What is your individual WHY? What is your organization's WHY? Does your WHY fit in, like a spoke in a wheel, to the greater WHY of the organization?

▶ Do you own what you sell? How much so? Does your product/service align with your WHY?

▶ Who is in charge of your organization's client experience?

▶ How many times a week does your team go beyond the business at hand—or make meaning—with clients? How might it happen with greater frequency and quality? What are some specific ways to create more "MOMM" with your clients?

▶ What else would you have had Funkhauzer say in his final speech?

▶ Are you aware of your strengths and weaknesses as a public speaker? When do you shine the most brightly in your speeches/presentations?

▶ What is your process for preparation for any given public speech?

▶ What does too much vulnerability, or too little, feel like in a speech?

▶ How much personal energy do you have right now? Is it in alignment with your WHY? How would you create more energy for yourself?

▶ Why is asking for advice so powerful for impact? Will you make it a habit for your organization?

▶ Is purity of purpose a realistic goal for emissaries of your organization?

For additional resources and expanded content, please visit:
TheTakeawayBook.com/Resources

Acknowledgments

"Everything in good fiction is a proper reassembly of reality."

— GREAT-GRANDPAPPY OTIS FUNKHAUZER

- ✌ Thanks to my wife, Alyson McGillicuddy Evans. Incapable of insincerity, she's my most important editor.

- ✌ Special acknowledgment to Anne Kvanbeck and David Master of Janus Henderson Investors, an incredible culture. Thank you for your trust.

Made in the USA
Columbia, SC
06 October 2021